EL SALVADOR

By Sloane Gould
and Alicia Z. Klepeis

Published in 2026 by Cavendish Square Publishing, LLC
2544 Clinton Street, Buffalo, NY 14224

Second Edition

Website: cavendishsq.com

Library of Congress Cataloging-in-Publication Data

Names: Gould, Sloane, author. | Klepeis, Alicia, author.
Title: El Salvador / by Sloane Gould and Alicia Z. Klepeis.
Description: Second edition. | New York : Cavendish Square Publishing, 2026. | Series: Exploring world cultures | Includes index.
Identifiers: LCCN 2024040851 (print) | LCCN 2024040852 (ebook) | ISBN 9781502673541 (library binding) | ISBN 9781502673534 (paperback) | ISBN 9781502673558 (ebook)
Subjects: LCSH: El Salvador--Juvenile literature.
Classification: LCC F1483.2 .K54 2026 (print) | LCC F1483.2 (ebook) | DDC 972.84--dc23/eng/20241228
LC record available at https://lccn.loc.gov/2024040851
LC ebook record available at https://lccn.loc.gov/2024040852

Writers: Alicia Z. Klepeis; Sloane Gould (second edition)
Editor: Caitie McAneney
Copyeditor: Jill Keppeler
Designer: Deanna Lepovich

The photographs in this book are used by permission and through the courtesy of: Cover edfuentesg/iStock.com; p. 4 tunasalmon/Shutterstock.com; p. 5 Ian MacLellan/Shutterstock.com; p. 6 Gianfranco Vivi/Shutterstock.com; p. 7 Rick100/Shutterstock.com; p. 8 Bosiljka Zutich/Alamy Stock Photo; p. 9 WitR/Shutterstock.com; p. 10 em_concepts/Shutterstock.com; p. 11 Milosz Maslanka/Shutterstock.com; pp. 12, 26 Omri Eliyahu/Shutterstock.com; p. 13 nanii212/Shutterstock.com; p. 14 Ondrej Prosicky/Shutterstock.com; pp. 15, 16 Galyna Andrushko/Shutterstock.com; pp. 17, 23 Gonzalo Bell/Shutterstock.com; pp. 18, 19 Alexandre Laprise/Shutterstock.com; pp. 20, 22 Elena Berd/Shutterstock.com; p. 21 Ivan Manzano/Shutterstock.com; p. 24 ponce.sv/Shutterstock.com; p. 25 Paulo Afonso/Shutterstock.com; p. 27 Luis.photoM95/Shutterstock.com; p. 28 AS Foodstudio/Shutterstock.com; p. 29 SALMONNEGRO-STOCK/Shutterstock.com.

CPSIA compliance information: Batch #CS26CSQ: For further information contact Cavendish Square Publishing LLC at 1-877-980-4450.

Printed in the United States of America

CONTENTS

INTRODUCTION

El Salvador is a Central American country with rich cultures, **traditions**, and landscapes. Called the "Land of Volcanoes," El Salvador is often under **threat** of earthquakes and volcanic activity. It's also home to mountains, rainforests, and freshwater lakes. People love to visit El Salvador's beautiful beaches. The rainforest is home to amazing plants such as orchids and amazing animals such as jaguars and toucans.

El Salvador is the smallest Central American country.

Today's El Salvador shows signs of its past as a home of the Maya **civilization** as well as a Spanish **colony**. Today, it is a free country, though many people there often deal with hardship and **violence**. Many people live in the countryside, while others live in large cities like San Salvador. The people who live in this country enjoy music, soccer, and special celebrations. Let's take a visit to the Land of Volcanoes—El Salvador!

People from El Salvador are called Salvadorans.

GEOGRAPHY

El Salvador is slighter smaller than the U.S. state of Massachusetts. El Salvador covers 8,124 square miles (21,041 sq km). Its southern side is on the coast of the Pacific Ocean. Honduras lies to the north and east. Guatemala borders El Salvador to the northwest.

FACT!

Unlike other Central American countries, El Salvador is not on the Caribbean Sea.

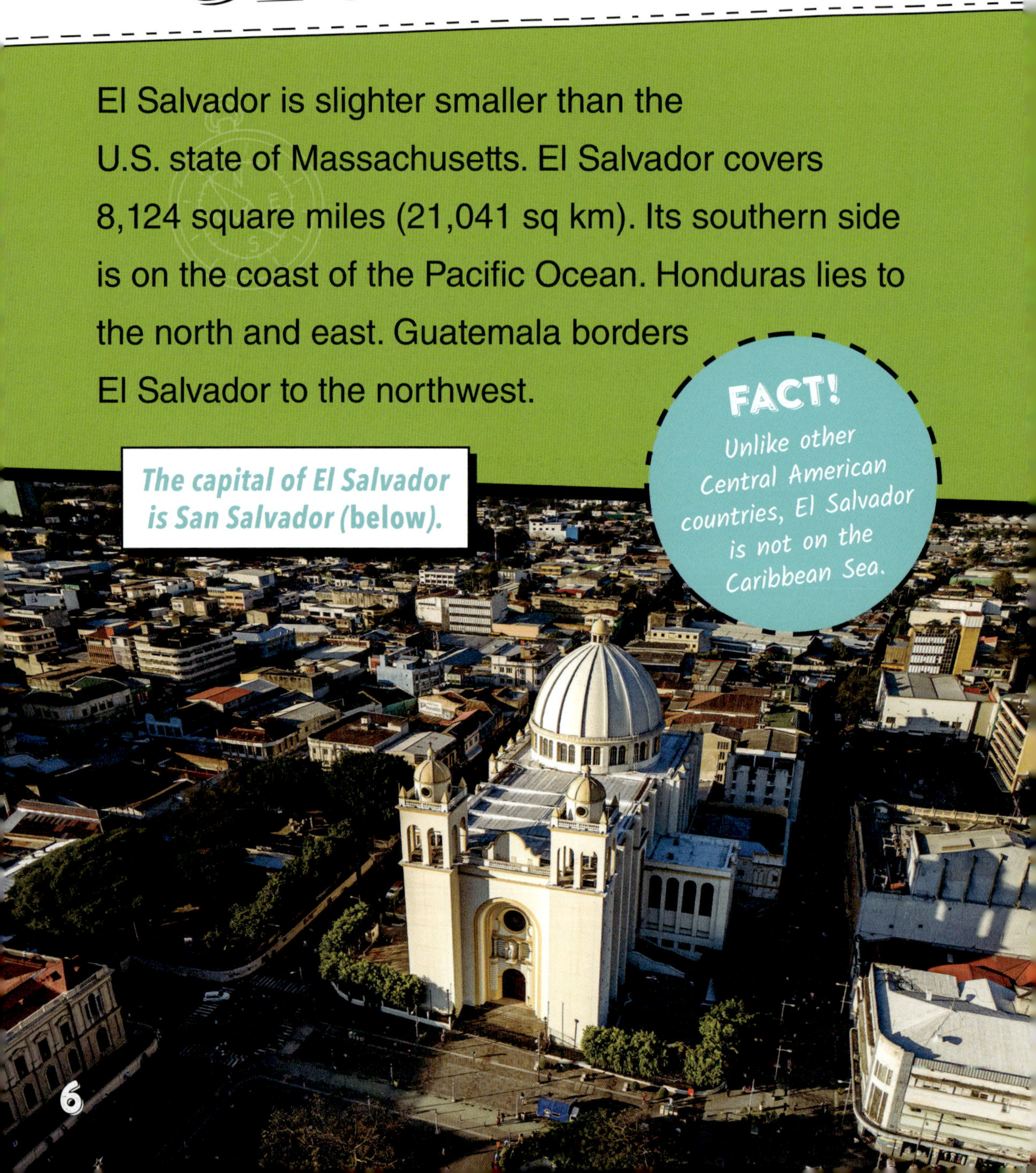

The capital of El Salvador is San Salvador (below).

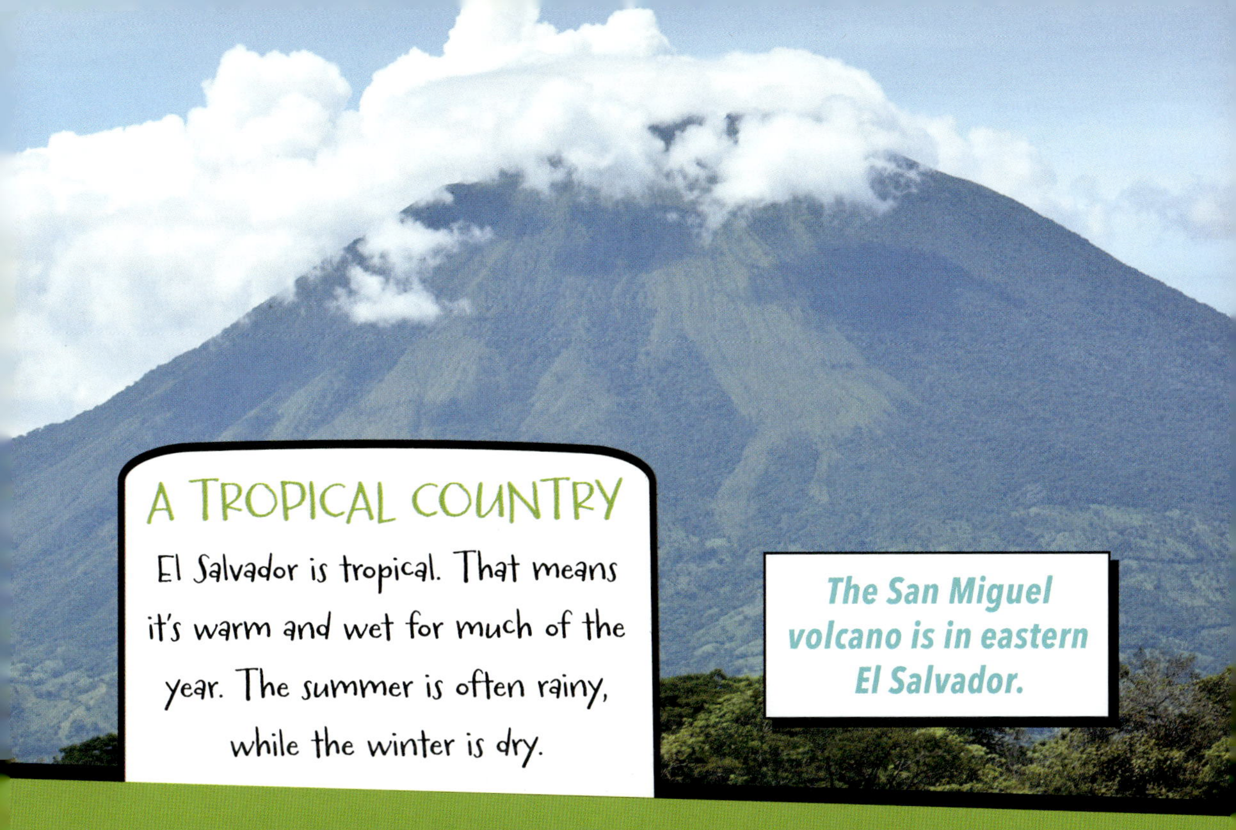

A TROPICAL COUNTRY

El Salvador is tropical. That means it's warm and wet for much of the year. The summer is often rainy, while the winter is dry.

The San Miguel volcano is in eastern El Salvador.

The country's largest river, the Lempa, runs through northwestern and central El Salvador. It's an important source of fresh water for the country. Most Salvadorans live in the middle of the country on a high, flat area called a plateau.

El Salvador's southern coast has flat plains with many farms. The Sierra Madre, a mountain range, is found in northern El Salvador. El Salvador has many active volcanoes. A volcano named San Miguel last erupted, giving off ash and gas, in 2023.

HISTORY

El Salvador had a long history before Europeans arrived. It was home to rich civilizations such as the Olmec, Maya, Toltec, and Pipil.

Spanish explorers came to El Salvador in the 1500s. The country was controlled by Spain until 1821. From 1823 to 1840, El Salvador was part of a federation with Honduras, Nicaragua, Guatemala, and Costa Rica. It broke up in 1840. El Salvador became independent.

Shown here is part of a stone decorated by ancient peoples in El Salvador.

In the 1850s, Salvadorans began to grow coffee, which brought many jobs. Coffee farmers had lots of power over the government. This caused great differences between the rich and those in **poverty**, which is called economic inequality. Poverty, **conflict**, and **gangs** are continuing problems in El Salvador.

Archbishop Óscar Romero fought for human rights in El Salvador. Human rights are the rights every person should have no matter what.

FACT!

*One important historical site, or place, is Joya de Cerén, an **ancient** farming community that was buried when a volcano erupted in 600 CE.*

CIVIL WAR

Because of economic inequality, a civil war broke out in 1980. This is war between two groups in a country. Around 75,000 people died before it ended in 1992.

GOVERNMENT

People in El Salvador vote for their leaders. Governments that allow their people to vote for leaders to represent them are called republics. A president is elected every five years.

The flag of El Salvador has two blue stripes with a white stripe in the middle. The white stripe has the country's ***crest.***

THE DEPARTMENTS OF EL SALVADOR

El Salvador has 14 departments, which are like states. The department with the most people is San Salvador.

El Salvador's government has three parts: legislative, judicial, and executive. The legislative, or lawmaking, part is called the Legislative Assembly. The executive part is made up of the president and the cabinet. Its members help the president run the government. The judicial part is made up of courts. The courts decide how to apply the laws. They follow the country's constitution, which was adopted in 1983. It describes all the basic laws of El Salvador. The government meets in the capital of San Salvador.

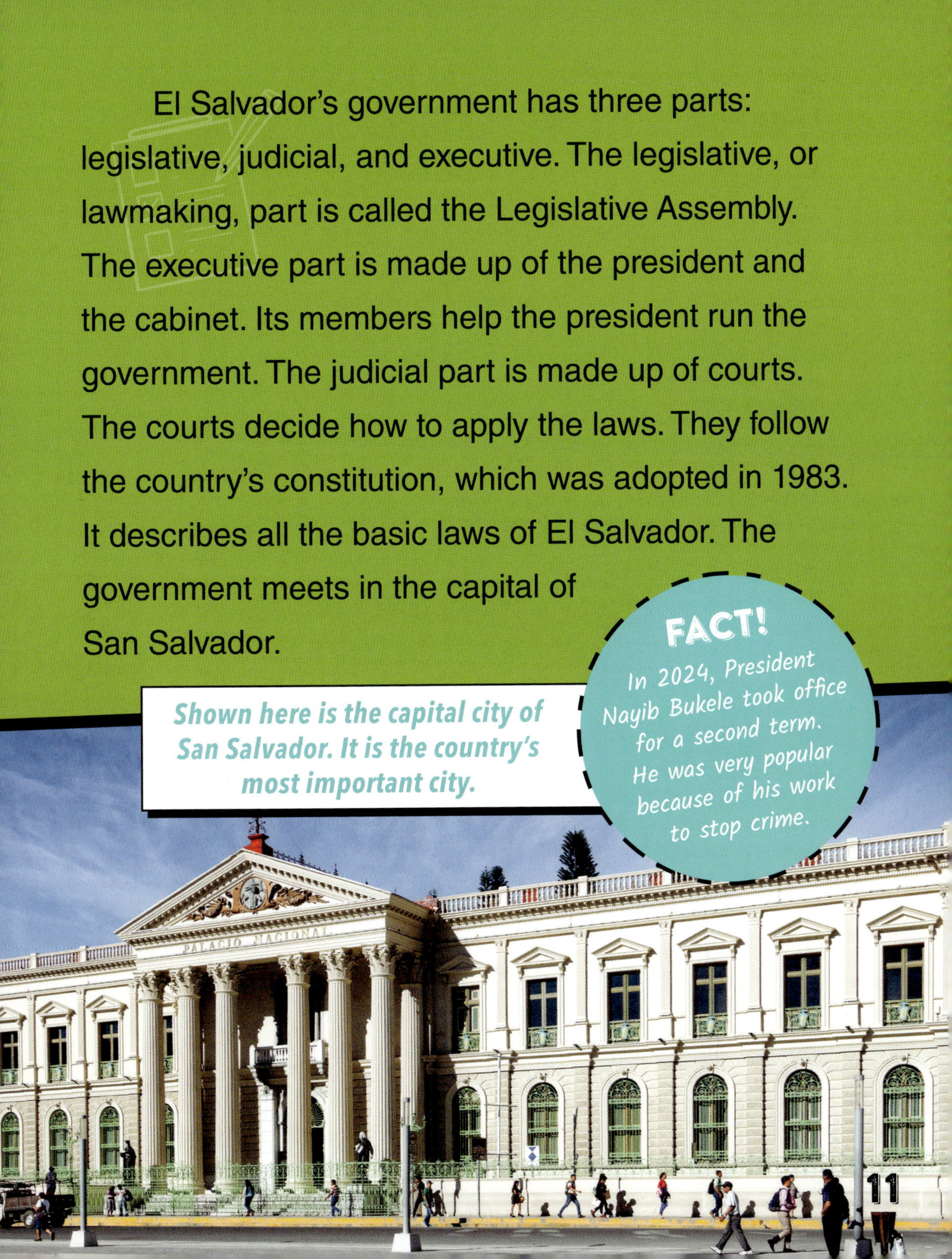

FACT!

In 2024, President Nayib Bukele took office for a second term. He was very popular because of his work to stop crime.

Shown here is the capital city of San Salvador. It is the country's most important city.

THE ECONOMY

El Salvador has a long history of farming and trade. However, the country often struggles with natural disasters, crime, and poverty. At least 20 percent of Salvadorans live in other countries. Many of them send some of the money they make back to their families in El Salvador.

FACT!

Salvadoran factories also produce petroleum, which is a kind of oil used for fuel.

People shop in this busy market in Nahuizalco, El Salvador.

El Salvador trades with countries like the United States, Honduras, Guatemala, and China. Factory workers in El Salvador make many different products, such as clothing and furniture. Farmers grow crops such as maize (corn), sugarcane, and beans.

Some Salvadorans work in banks, hospitals, restaurants, and offices. Tourism, or people visiting from other countries, is important to the economy in San Salvador and coastal areas known for surfing and beautiful beaches.

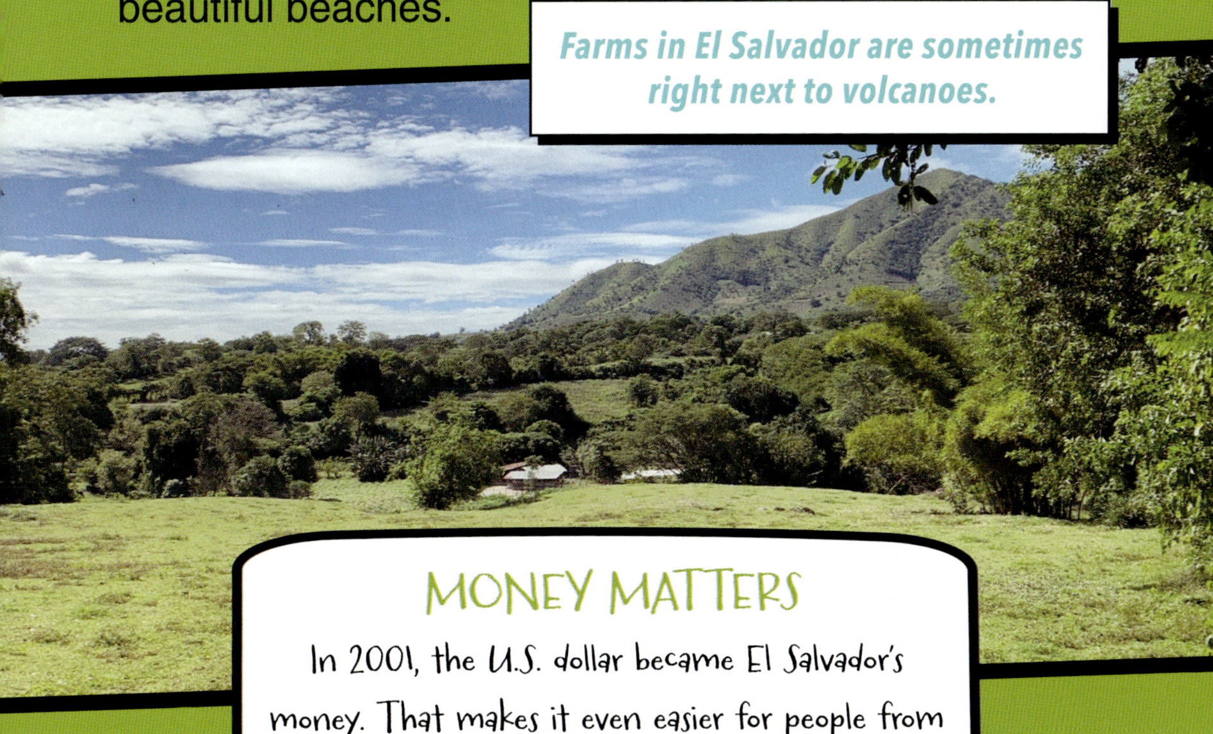

Farms in El Salvador are sometimes right next to volcanoes.

MONEY MATTERS

In 2001, the U.S. dollar became El Salvador's money. That makes it even easier for people from the United States to visit and buy from El Salvador.

THE ENVIRONMENT

Like other Central American countries, El Salvador is full of natural beauty. Its coastline and rainforest areas are home to many kinds of plants and animals. Coconut and palm trees grow along the southern coast. Armadillos, snakes, and iguanas live near the coast too. Grasses, small trees, and bushes cover the central plains, which are home to white-tailed deer. Pine and oak trees grow in the mountains. Animals such as spider monkeys, jaguars, and anteaters live in the forests.

Wild cats live in the rainforest of El Salvador.

El Salvador has faced environmental issues, or harm to its natural landscapes, such as deforestation. Many water sources are unsafe because farms and factories **pollute** them. Luckily, cleaner sources of power—from wind, sun, and water—are becoming more popular in El Salvador. National parks are safe spaces for animals in this country.

FACT!

El Salvador has birds such as toucans, herons, pelicans, and wild ducks.

DEFORESTATION

Many forests in El Salvador have been cut down for firewood and farming. This is called deforestation. This means animals lose their homes.

This view shows Cerro Verde National Park in El Salvador.

THE PEOPLE TODAY

El Salvador is home to about 6.6 million people. Many of them live near the capital city of San Salvador. It is a very crowded city, with more than 1 million people. The average person in El Salvador can expect a lifespan of around 75 years.

This Native person shares music in San Salvador.

INDIGENOUS PEOPLES

Only 0.2 percent of Salvadorans are Indigenous, or native to the region. Indigenous groups include the Lenca, Kakawira, and Nahea-Pipil peoples.

More than 86 percent of Salvadorans are mestizo. The second-largest group in El Salvador is white people. They make up around 13 percent of the country's population.

FACT!

Mestizo means having both Native and European backgrounds.

More than 100,000 people of Palestinian ancestry, or backgrounds, live in El Salvador. In February 2019, El Salvador elected a president with Palestinian ancestry—Nayib Bukele. Many Palestinians came to the country in the early 20th century looking for new opportunities.

Clean drinking water can increase a person's lifespan. Clean drinking water is often scarce, or hard to get, in El Salvador.

LIFESTYLE

Life in El Salvador is different for people who have enough money and those who don't. People with a lot of money often live in the city in houses or apartments. They often work in or around the city.

FACT!

About 46 percent of Salvadoran women work.

Many people sleep or rest in hammocks in El Salvador.

SALVADORAN SCHOOLS

School is free in El Salvador, but many people struggle to get to school or pay for school supplies. Still, more than 70 percent of Salvadorans finish middle school.

Those without enough money often live a very different lifestyle in cities. Some people live in shacks made of sheet metal and plastic. Many homes have too many people living in them. Crime and gangs are problems in El Salvador's cities.

Salvadoran families often have about two children.

In the countryside, Salvadorans often work on farms. Homes here are typically made of **adobe**, wood, or concrete blocks. Many do not have electricity or running water. Life is hard. People often walk or travel by pickup trucks or buses. It's possible to get around much of El Salvador on a bus.

RELIGION

The history of religion, or faith, in El Salvador is shown in its name, which comes from the Spanish word for "savior." This refers to Jesus Christ, the main figure in Christianity. Christianity was brought to Central America by the Spanish. The Christian religion is important for many Salvadorans. Nearly all of El Salvador's national holidays, such as Christmas, are Christian. In fact, it is one of the only countries to celebrate the Christian holiday of Easter for four days, from Thursday to Sunday.

El Salvador has many churches.

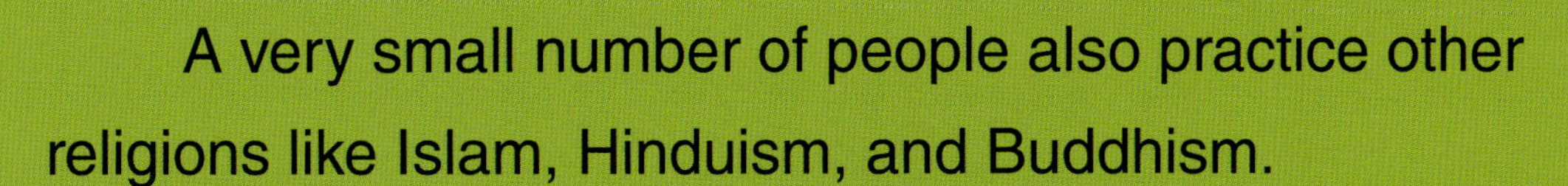

A very small number of people also practice other religions like Islam, Hinduism, and Buddhism. El Salvador has no official religion. People are free to believe what they want. Some Salvadorans do not follow any religion.

FACT!

Archbishop Óscar Romero was killed in 1980 and became a saint (an important Catholic figure) in 2018.

Óscar Romero's tomb, or final resting place, is at the Metropolitan Cathedral of San Salvador.

RELIGIOUS CELEBRATIONS

The Festival of El Salvador del Mundo takes place each August. It celebrates El Salvador del Mundo (the Savior of the World). There are parades, street parties, and other fun events.

LANGUAGE

El Salvador's history as a Spanish colony is seen in its religion. It's also seen in its language. Today, Spanish is still the language of El Salvador. The government uses Spanish. Businesspeople also use Spanish.

A small number of Salvadorans still speak Indigenous languages. Nawat, also known as Pipil, is one example. Unfortunately, this language is in danger of dying out because there are so few speakers.

FACT!

Many Native Salvadorans spoke Nawat before the 20th century. However, it was outlawed from 1932 to 2014.

This sign in El Boquerón National Park has both Spanish and English on it.

Other languages are used in El Salvador. Caliche is a kind of Spanish spoken in El Salvador and other parts of Central America. It includes words and phrases from Indigenous languages. English is the most popular foreign language taught in Salvadoran schools. People also sometimes speak English for work. Salvadoran Sign Language became a recognized language in 2005.

TEACHING NAWAT

Some communities in El Salvador are teaching Nawat to children in school to try to save it. The hope is that people will continue to speak Nawat in the future.

Kids in El Salvador have their school lessons in Spanish.

ARTS AND FESTIVALS

Salvadoran art is often full of color. Artist Fernando Llort created colorful folk art that mixed Maya and modern styles. Many art pieces from El Salvador have the bright colors and simple shapes that Llort used in his art. Because of this, Llort has been called El Salvador's national artist.

FACT!
El Salvador is known for colorful handmade hammocks and blankets.

El Salvador is known for its colorful masks, which are worn in parades and festivals.

Folk art makes its way into pottery too. The town of Ilobacso is known for pottery, especially *sorpresas*, or surprises. They have colorful tops. Hidden underneath are figures of people doing daily tasks like working or cooking.

Salvadoran churches are kinds of art.

Salvadorans celebrate their independence from Spain on September 15. There are parades and fireworks. At another event, the Festival of Palms and Flowers in Panchimalco, people create beautiful flower arrangements and have parades.

MUSIC IN EL SALVADOR

There are many styles of music in El Salvador. Cumbia is popular. It has a bouncy feel to it. Chanchona music comes from the eastern part of the country.

FUN AND PLAY

There are many ways to have fun in El Salvador. Many people simply enjoy the tropical surroundings. Many Salvadorans spent lots of time outside. Both locals and tourists enjoy hiking in El Salvador's national parks or camping in the mountains. In the waters on the coast, people like surfing and swimming. Fishing is another common activity.

FACT!

Many people hike in the tropical forest in El Salvador's El Imposible National Park.

Many people enjoy surfing at El Tunco beach in El Salvador.

A *capirucho* is a traditional toy in El Salvador. Children toss the bell-shaped part of the toy in the air and try to catch it on the handle.

Soccer is the most popular sport in the country. Both kids and adults play. People in El Salvador also love watching soccer in person and on TV. Many cheer on the national *futbol* (soccer) team of El Salvador at Estadio Cuscatlán. It's one of the biggest **stadiums** in Central America.

Estadio Cuscatlán is in San Salvador.

SALVADORAN OLYMPIANS

Salvadorans have competed in the Olympics since 1968. In the 2024 Summer Olympics, they competed in archery, badminton, and judo as well as water sports such as swimming, sailing, and surfing.

FOOD

If you go to El Salvador, you may want to try one of their specialties—a *pupusa*. Pupusas are a popular street food. They are corn tortillas stuffed with beans, meat, or cheese. People eat them as a snack or even a light meal.

The three most common things in Salvadoran cooking are tortillas, rice, and beans. Meat is expensive, so most people in El Salvador rely on these staples instead. Tropical fruits are also added to meals for color and flavor.

Street vendors, or sellers, sell pupusas in San Salvador.

Coffee, soda, and fruit juices are all popular drinks in El Salvador. Salvadorans enjoy desserts too. A *semita* is a pastry often filled with pineapple jam. *Empanadas de platano* are desserts made of plantain dough and stuffed with custard.

FACT!

Atol de elote is a drink made of fresh corn, sugar, milk, salt and cinnamon.

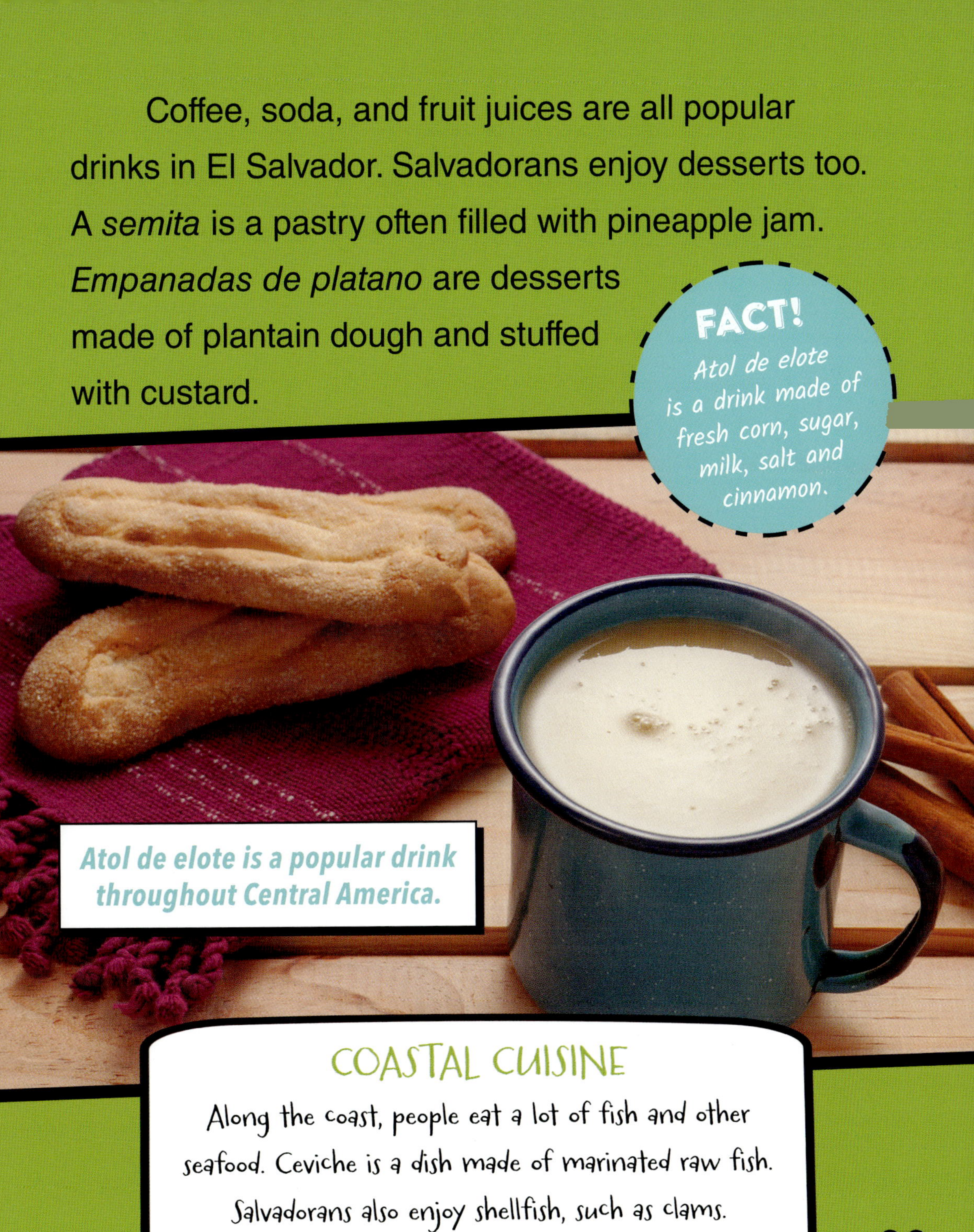

Atol de elote is a popular drink throughout Central America.

COASTAL CUISINE

Along the coast, people eat a lot of fish and other seafood. Ceviche is a dish made of marinated raw fish. Salvadorans also enjoy shellfish, such as clams.

GLOSSARY

adobe: A building material or brick made of earth and straw.

archbishop: A high-ranking member of the Catholic Church.

ancient: Having to do with something or someone from long ago.

civilization: An organized society with written records and laws.

colony: A piece of land under the control of another country.

conflict: A fight, battle, or war.

crest: A special picture that stands for a country or group.

gang: A group of people working together in unlawful activity.

pollute: To make something unsafe or unhealthy with waste made by humans.

poverty: The state of being poor.

stadium: A large gathering place where sports teams play.

threat: Something likely to cause harm.

tradition: Something that's been done for a long time.

violence: The use of force to harm someone.

FIND OUT MORE

Books

Barghoorn, Linda. *A Refugee's Journey from El Salvador*. St. Catharine's, ON: Crabtree Publishing Company, 2022.

González, Cynthia. *The Life Of Llort*. Los Angeles, CA: Lil' Libros, 2022.

Katstaller, Rachel. *Itzel and the Ocelot*. Toronto, ON: Kids Can Press, 2022.

Websites

El Salvador
kids.britannica.com/students/article/El-Salvador/274167
Discover more interesting facts about El Salvador with Britannica.

Rainforest Habitat
kids.nationalgeographic.com/nature/habitats/article/rain-forest
Learn more about rainforest habitats with *National Geographic Kids*.

Video

Ancient Mayan Facts for Kids
www.youtube.com/watch?v=Q7lIX0YGlsw
Learn more about the ancient Maya civilization in this video.

Publisher's note to educators and parents: Our editors have carefully reviewed these websites to ensure that they are suitable for students. Many websites change frequently, however, and we cannot guarantee that a site's future contents will continue to meet our high standards of quality and educational value. Be advised that students should be closely supervised whenever they access the internet.

INDEX